I0663308

Lost Hearts

*A Chilling Tale of Dark Rituals and
Ghostly Revenge*

A Modern Translation

Adapted for the Contemporary Reader

M.R. James

Translated by Tim Zengerink

Table of Contents

Preface - Message to the Reader

What If You Could Help Rebuild the Greatest Library in Human History?

Thousands of years ago, the Library of Alexandria stood as the crown jewel of human achievement — a sanctuary where the collected wisdom of every known civilization was gathered, preserved, and shared freely.

And then, it was lost.

Through fire, conquest, and the slow erosion of time, humanity lost not just books — but ideas, dreams, discoveries, and stories that could have changed the world forever.

Today, the Library of Alexandria lives again — and you are invited to be a part of its restoration.

Our mission is simple yet profound:

To rebuild the greatest library the world has ever known, and to translate all timeless works into every language and dialect, so that no seeker of knowledge is ever left behind again.

By joining our movement to rebuild the modern Library of Alexandria, you become part of an unprecedented mission:

- **Unlimited Access to the Greatest Audiobooks & eBooks Ever Written:**

  Instantly explore thousands of legendary works—Plato, Shakespeare, Jane Austen, Leo Tolstoy, and countless more. All instantly available to read or listen, placing a complete literary universe at your fingertips.

- **Beautiful Paperback & Deluxe Editions at Printing Cost**

  Own any title as an elegant paperback, deluxe hardcover, or stunning collectible boxset—offered to you at true printing cost, delivered straight to your door. Build your personal Library of Alexandria, crafted for beauty, built for durability, and worthy of proud display.

- **Fresh Translations for Modern Readers—in Every Language & Dialect**

  Enjoy timeless masterpieces reimagined in clear, contemporary language—no more outdated phrases or obscure references. Alongside the original versions, we're tirelessly translating these classics into every language and dialect imaginable, ensuring accessibility and understanding across cultures and generations.

- **Join a Global Renaissance of Literature & Knowledge**

  You directly support expanding our library, publishing deluxe editions at true cost, translating works into all global languages, and bringing humanity's greatest stories to people everywhere. By joining today, you're not just preserving a legacy of masterpieces; you set in motion a powerful wave of literary accessibility.

Become a Torchbearer of Knowledge.

Join us for free now at **LibraryofAlexandria.com**

Together, we will ensure that the light of human wisdom never fades again.

With gratitude and a shared love of knowledge,

The Modern Library of Alexandria Team

Visit:

www.libraryofalexandria.com

Or scan the code below:

Introduction

M.R. James, the Scholarly Ghost Story, and the Terrifying Power of Innocence

M.R. James's Lost Hearts, first published in 1895, is a masterwork of the ghost story genre: concise, elegant, and disturbingly effective. At just under 4,000 words, the story seems almost modest in length, but its impact is far-reaching. It remains one of the most frequently anthologized of James's tales and stands as a chilling example of his unique ability to weave horror into the familiar landscapes of English antiquarianism and domestic life. What makes Lost Hearts so unsettling is not merely its spectral apparitions or the uncanny atmosphere James conjures, but the disturbing moral undercurrent that runs beneath its surface—one that involves exploitation, betrayal, and the destruction of childhood innocence in the name of occult ambition.

In contrast to the later Gothic novels that paint horror with heavy strokes of melodrama, James perfected what he called the "antiquarian ghost story"— a form grounded in realistic settings, scholarly characters, and slow-building dread rather than overt sensationalism. Lost Hearts is among his earliest published stories, written while he was still Provost of King's College, Cambridge. It features all the hallmarks of Jamesian horror: a reclusive scholar, ancient esoteric texts, an isolated country estate, and supernatural vengeance that comes not through random haunting, but as a direct consequence of human sin.

The tale follows a young orphan named Stephen Elliott, who is sent to live with his distant cousin Mr. Abney, an eccentric scholar obsessed with immortality. Abney seems kindly and welcoming, but beneath his polite exterior lies a sinister motive: he is engaged in arcane research involving the sacrifice of children to achieve eternal life. Stephen, unknowingly selected as Abney's next victim, begins to experience strange visions and ghostly manifestations of two other children—his would-be predecessors—whose hearts were taken for Abney's experiments. The horror of the story builds not through gore, but through the dawning realization of what Abney has done, and what he intends to do again.

This introduction will explore the themes, structure, and significance of Lost Hearts within M.R. James's oeuvre and within the broader tradition of supernatural fiction. We will examine how James constructs atmosphere, uses restraint as a weapon of narrative power, and critiques intellectual hubris through horror. We will also explore the role of childhood, innocence, and justice in the tale's ultimate revenge. Though written in an age of spiritualism and scientific optimism, Lost Hearts remains a timeless meditation on the consequences of ambition without morality—and a terrifying reminder that the past, especially when it involves the unjustly silenced, never stays buried for long.

Antiquarian Horrors:
Rational Men, Occult Obsessions,
and the Rise of the Scholarly Ghost Story

M.R. James was not only a master of the ghost story— he was also a medievalist, biblical scholar, and antiquarian with a passion for dusty manuscripts, cathedral libraries, and historical minutiae. His fiction reflects this intellectual world, and Lost Hearts is no exception. Set in an 1811 Lincolnshire manor house, the story is steeped in antiquity, from its arcane references to Greek mystery cults to its protagonist's status as an independently wealthy but isolated scholar. Mr. Abney, the villain of the piece, is a Jamesian archetype: reclusive, learned, and dangerously curious.

Abney's interest in the occult, specifically the idea that the hearts of children can grant longevity and supernatural power, draws upon historical traditions of dark alchemy and folk magic. James never invents entire mythologies like Lovecraft would later do; rather, he draws on fragments of real esoteric lore, grounding his horror in plausible arcane belief. Abney's research feels authentic, and that realism enhances the dread. His diary entries, which reveal the true nature of his actions, are rendered in the calm, scholarly tone of an academic footnote—an intentional and chilling contrast to the abominable nature of his deeds.

This fusion of erudition and evil is central to James's unique brand of horror. Unlike Gothic villains who shriek and curse, Abney is rational and polite. His crimes are couched in scholarship and framed as metaphysical experimentation. This, perhaps, is the most disturbing element of the story: the suggestion that knowledge without conscience is not just dangerous—it is monstrous. Abney treats children not as human beings, but as ingredients in a formula. His library, once a symbol of wisdom, becomes a laboratory of murder.

The figure of the "scholar-gone-wrong" recurs throughout James's fiction and speaks to a broader Victorian anxiety about the limits of reason. The late

19th century was a period of tremendous scientific and academic advancement, but also of spiritual dislocation. In Lost Hearts, James critiques the idea that human beings, in pursuit of forbidden knowledge, can violate the natural order without consequence. The ghosts that return to torment Abney are not senseless apparitions—they are symbols of moral reckoning. Their silent presence is not only terrifying—it is just.

Child Victims and Silent Revenge: Justice in the Ghost Story

One of the most striking aspects of Lost Hearts is its use of children as both victims and agents of supernatural revenge. In many traditional ghost stories, children are the ones to be frightened. In James's story, they are the ones who return to terrify—and ultimately to destroy—the adult who wronged them. This reversal gives Lost Hearts a deep emotional resonance. The story does not dwell on the gruesome details of the murders, but its implications are horrifying. The fact that Abney removes their hearts is never depicted graphically, but the very phrase "lost hearts" is chilling in its quiet finality.

The ghosts of the two murdered children are not aggressive or demonic. They are mournful, eerie, and persistent. Their appearances to Stephen are atmospheric rather than confrontational: the sound of scratching at the window, a glimpse of long fingernails, a thin figure in nightclothes, a whimpering voice. These details are not simply scary—they are profoundly sad. James never sensationalizes their suffering. Instead, he lets their sorrow speak louder than their screams.

The climax of the story occurs offstage. Abney dies suddenly, and his servant finds him mutilated—his chest torn open, presumably by the spirits of the children. James offers no direct description of the attack, only the aftermath and a cryptic diary entry. This narrative restraint is typical of James and is part of what makes Lost Hearts so effective. The horror is in the suggestion, the implication. What we imagine is always worse than what is shown.

The revenge of the ghosts is swift, silent, and absolute. They do not haunt Stephen. They do not linger. Once Abney is gone, they disappear. Their business is done. In this, James allows for a form of poetic justice. The supernatural, in his fiction, often operates not as chaos, but as moral correction. The ghosts are not evil—they are restorers of balance. This structure makes the story satisfying as well as frightening. The horror has a point. The wrongs are avenged. The innocent are freed.

And yet, the story does not end on triumph. The final image—of a boy narrowly saved from a terrible fate, surrounded by the lingering shadows of death—reminds us that evil is not always obvious. It can wear the face of kindness, speak in the voice of reason, and reside in the places we think are safest. The real terror of Lost Hearts is not the ghosts.

It is the fact that a learned man, respected and genteel, could murder children in secret—and almost succeed.

Legacy and the Lasting Influence of Lost Hearts

Lost Hearts is one of M.R. James's earliest stories, but it already demonstrates the masterful control and intellectual subtlety that would define his later work. It stands as a cornerstone of modern supernatural fiction, influencing generations of writers from Robert Aickman and Shirley Jackson to Stephen King and Susan Hill. Its blend of antiquarian detail, psychological horror, and restrained narrative remains a model for how to craft effective and enduring ghost stories.

James's legacy lies not only in the chills his stories provoke, but in the ethical questions they raise. Lost Hearts is not a story about ghosts—it is a story about what happens when human beings try to escape the consequences of their actions. It is about how the dead can speak truth more powerfully than the living. And it is about how innocence, even when destroyed, can rise again—not to haunt, but to judge.

In this way, Lost Hearts transcends its genre. It becomes more than a tale of terror. It becomes a parable—a warning about the dangers of intellectual arrogance, the cost of unchecked ambition, and the enduring power of the voiceless to speak from beyond the grave.

For readers today, Lost Hearts still holds its grip, not just through its spectral images or atmospheric dread, but through the quiet, moral clarity that lies beneath its horror. It asks us to consider not only what frightens us, but what we have chosen not to see. And in doing so, it reminds us that the worst monsters are not always the ones that come in the night.

Sometimes, they sit in libraries. They offer us tea. They smile. And they wait.

Lost Hearts

As far as I can tell, it was sometime in September of 1811 when a small carriage stopped in front of Aswarby Hall, deep in the countryside of Lincolnshire. The only passenger, a young boy, quickly jumped out and looked around with wide-eyed curiosity while waiting for someone to answer the doorbell.

In front of him stood a tall, square house made of red brick, built during Queen Anne's time. A porch with stone columns, added later in 1790, gave the house a more classical look. The house had many tall, narrow windows with small glass panes and thick white frames. A triangle-shaped piece with a round window at the top sat above the front entrance.

On both sides of the main house were wings, connected to the center by covered walkways with glass walls and columns. These side buildings clearly held the stables and service rooms. Each one was topped with a decorative dome and a golden weather vane.

The setting sun cast a warm light across the building, making the windows glow like tiny fires. In front of the house stretched a flat park, scattered with oak trees and bordered by tall firs. In the distance, a church tower hidden among trees marked the edge of the park, and its golden weathercock caught the sunlight. The church clock struck six, and the sound floated gently through the air. The boy waiting on the doorstep felt a mix of calm and sadness, the kind of feeling that often comes on early autumn evenings.

The carriage had brought him from Warwickshire. About six months earlier, he had lost both parents and become an orphan. His older cousin, Mr. Abney, had kindly offered to take him in, which surprised many people. Those who knew anything about Mr. Abney thought of him as a serious, private man who lived a quiet, structured life. A lively young boy seemed out of place in his home.

In truth, not much was known about Mr. Abney's personality or interests. A professor from Cambridge had once said that no one understood the old religions of the pagans better than Mr. Abney. His library was filled with rare books about ancient mysteries, the Orphic poems, the god Mithras, and Neo-Platonism. In the entrance hall, there was an impressive statue showing Mithras killing a bull. Mr. Abney had bought it from overseas at great cost. He even wrote about it in a popular magazine and published several articles about Roman superstitions. He was known for being deeply involved in his studies, so it came as a shock when he not only remembered his orphaned cousin, Stephen Elliott, but also invited him to live at Aswarby Hall.

Despite what people expected, Mr. Abney—the tall, thin, serious man—seemed happy to welcome Stephen. The moment the door opened, he came rushing out of his study, rubbing his hands together with excitement.

"How are you, my boy? How are you? How old are you?" he asked. "I hope your trip didn't make you too tired to eat?"

"No, thank you, sir. I'm feeling fine," Stephen replied.

"Good boy!" said Mr. Abney. "And how old are you, again?"

It was a little strange that he had asked that question twice so quickly.

"I'll be twelve on my next birthday, sir," Stephen answered.

"And when's your birthday, my dear boy? The eleventh of September? That's good—very good. That's nearly a year from now, isn't it? I like to write these things down in my book. You're sure it's twelve? Absolutely sure?"

"Yes, I'm sure, sir."

"Good, good! Parkes, take him to Mrs. Bunch's room and let him have some supper or tea, whatever's ready."

"Yes, sir," said Mr. Parkes, who spoke calmly and politely, then led Stephen down to the lower part of the house.

Mrs. Bunch turned out to be the kindest and most welcoming person Stephen had met at Aswarby so far. She made him feel right at home, and within fifteen minutes, they had already become good friends—and they stayed that way. Mrs. Bunch had lived in the area for fifty-five years and had worked at the Hall for twenty of them. So if anyone knew the history of the house and the surrounding area, it was her—and she was more than happy to share what she knew.

There were definitely a lot of things around the Hall and its gardens that Stephen, who was curious and liked to explore, wanted to understand. He had questions like, "Who built that little temple at the end of the laurel path?" and "Who was the old man in the painting on the staircase, the one sitting at a table with a skull beside him?" Mrs. Bunch, who was very knowledgeable, was able to answer many of these questions. But there were some things she didn't have such clear answers for.

One evening in November, Stephen was sitting by the fire in Mrs. Bunch's room, thinking about everything he had seen since arriving.

"Is Mr. Abney a good person? Do you think he'll go to heaven?" Stephen asked all of a sudden. He said it the way kids do—completely sure that adults know the answers to big, important questions.

"Oh, bless you, child!" Mrs. Bunch said. "The master is one of the kindest people I've ever known! Didn't I ever tell you about the little boy he took in off the street about seven years ago? And then the little girl, just two years after I started working here?"

"No, you haven't! Please tell me now, Mrs. Bunch!" Stephen said eagerly.

"Well," she began, "I don't remember too much about the little girl, to be honest. I just know the master brought her home with him after one of his walks and told Mrs. Ellis—she was the housekeeper back then—to take good care of her. The poor child didn't have any family. She told me that herself. She stayed here for about three weeks, I think. Then one morning, before anyone else had woken up, she was just gone. No one ever found out where she went. The master was very upset. He even had the ponds searched. But I've always believed that a group of traveling gypsies took her.

People heard singing near the house that night, and Parkes said he heard voices calling in the woods that afternoon. She was an odd little thing—quiet and different—but I liked her a lot. She was so gentle and peaceful, like she really fit in here."

"What about the boy?" Stephen asked.

"Oh, that poor lad," sighed Mrs. Bunch. "He wasn't from around here—he was a foreigner. Called himself Jevanny. He came one cold day playing his hurdy-gurdy along the drive. Master saw him, invited him in right away, and asked all about where he came from, how old he was, and if he had any family. Treated him very kindly. But it ended the same way. Just like the girl, he vanished one morning. We wondered for a long time why he left and where he went. He didn't even take his hurdy-gurdy—it's still sitting up on the shelf."

Stephen spent the rest of the evening asking Mrs. Bunch all sorts of questions and trying to get the hurdy-gurdy to play a tune.

That night, he had a strange dream.

At the end of the hallway upstairs, near his bedroom, there was old bathroom that no one used anymore. The door was locked, but the top half had a glass window. The curtains that used to cover it were long gone, so you could see inside. The bath was made of lead and attached to the wall on the right, with the head of it facing the window.

In his dream, Stephen found himself standing outside that door, looking in. The moonlight was shining through the window, and he could see something lying in the tub.

What he saw was frightening. It reminded me of what I once saw in the underground crypts of St. Michan's Church in Dublin, where old bodies don't rot for centuries. The figure in the dream was terribly thin, with grayish, dusty skin. It was wrapped in a cloth like a burial shroud. Its mouth was twisted into a faint, creepy smile, and its hands were tightly crossed over its chest.

As Stephen stared, he heard a soft, faraway moan come from the figure's lips. Then its arms slowly started to move.

The sight filled him with such fear that he stumbled backward—and woke up to find himself standing in the hallway, barefoot on the cold wooden floor, with the moonlight shining all around him.

Most boys would have run back to bed, but Stephen bravely walked to the bathroom door to check if what he saw was really there.

It wasn't. He quietly returned to bed.

The next morning, Mrs. Bunch was quite shaken by what Stephen had told her. She even went so far as to hang a curtain back over the glass panel in the old bathroom door. Mr. Abney, too, seemed very interested when Stephen told him about the dream during breakfast. He wrote everything down in what he called "his book."

As spring approached, Mr. Abney often reminded Stephen that the spring equinox was an important time, especially for young people—at least, according to the ancient writers he studied. He kept telling Stephen to take care of himself, to keep his bedroom window shut at night, and even mentioned that someone named Censorinus had written important things on the topic.

Two strange things happened around this time that Stephen couldn't stop thinking about.

The first happened after a night when Stephen had slept very badly. He felt uneasy all night, though he couldn't remember any dreams.

The next evening, Mrs. Bunch was sitting near the fire, fixing his nightshirt.

"Heavens, Master Stephen!" she said in frustration. "How do you tear your nightclothes like this? Look at the mess—poor servants like me have to fix all this!"

There were long, deep scratches on the left side of the fabric, as if something had sliced it again and again. Some of the cuts didn't go all the way through, but they would still take skill to repair. Stephen had no idea how they got there. He was sure they hadn't been there when he went to bed.

"But, Mrs. Bunch," he said, "they look exactly like the scratches on the outside of my bedroom door. And I know I didn't make those either."

Mrs. Bunch stared at him, then quickly grabbed a candle and hurried out of the room. Stephen heard her climbing the stairs. A few minutes later, she came back down.

"Well," she said, "Master Stephen, I can't imagine how those marks got there. They're too high up for any cat or dog, and definitely too high for a rat. They're just like what my uncle used to say about the fingernails of those men from China he met when he worked in the tea trade. If I were you, I wouldn't say anything to the master. Just make sure to lock your bedroom door at night."

"I always do, Mrs. Bunch, right after I say my prayers."

"That's good. Always say your prayers, and nothing can harm you."

With that, she went back to sewing the torn nightgown. She paused now and then, clearly thinking about what she'd seen. This happened on a Friday night in March, 1812.

The next night, Stephen and Mrs. Bunch were sitting together again, but this time their quiet evening was interrupted. Mr. Parkes, the butler, walked in unexpectedly. He usually kept to himself in his own area and rarely joined them. Tonight, though, he looked nervous and spoke faster than usual. He didn't even notice Stephen was there.

"If the master wants his wine in the evening, he can get it himself," Parkes said sharply. "I'll do it in the daytime, or not at all. I don't know what's going on— maybe it's rats, or maybe the wind's gotten into the cellar—but I'm not young anymore, and I can't deal with it like I used to."

"Well now, Mr. Parkes," said Mrs. Bunch, "everyone knows this place is full of rats. That's nothing new."

"I'm not saying it isn't, Mrs. Bunch. And I've heard stories from the shipyard men about talking rats, but I never believed any of it. Until tonight. If I had bent down and put my ear to the far bin, I swear I could've heard voices."

"Oh come on, Mr. Parkes," Mrs. Bunch snapped. "You expect me to believe rats are talking in the wine cellar? That's nonsense!"

"I'm not trying to start a fight," he said. "But if you want to prove it for yourself, go ahead. Go to the far bin, lean your ear against the door, and see if I'm wrong."

"What silly talk, Mr. Parkes! This is no story to be telling in front of children. You'll scare Master Stephen to death."

"What! Master Stephen's here?" Parkes suddenly realized. "Oh, well, he knows when I'm just having a bit of fun with you, Mrs. Bunch."

But Stephen wasn't fooled. He could tell Mr. Parkes hadn't been joking at first. The whole thing made him uneasy, though he was also curious. He tried asking more questions, hoping Parkes would explain what had really happened in the cellar—but the butler wouldn't say another word.

***

It was now March 24, 1812—a day full of strange moments for Stephen. The wind howled loudly, making the house and garden feel unsettled and uneasy. As he stood by the fence and looked out into the open park, he got the strange feeling that a crowd of invisible people were rushing past him, carried by the wind, as if trying to hold on to something and stop themselves—but unable to, lost and pushed forward without direction. It felt like they were trying to return to the world of the living, but couldn't.

After lunch that day, Mr. Abney said,

"Stephen, my boy, can you come to my study tonight at eleven? I'll be busy until then, but there's something important about your future I want to show you. Don't tell Mrs. Bunch or anyone else in the house. Just go to your room at the usual time, then come down quietly later."

Stephen was thrilled. Staying up late for a secret meeting felt like a new adventure. That evening, as he passed the library on his way upstairs, he peeked inside. The small metal fire bowl he had seen before had been moved in front of the fireplace. On the table stood a silver-gold cup filled with red wine, and beside it were several pages of writing. Mr. Abney was sprinkling some kind of incense onto the glowing coals from a round silver container, and didn't seem to notice Stephen at the door.

The wind had died down, and the sky was calm with a full moon. Around ten o'clock, Stephen stood at his bedroom window, staring out at the moonlit landscape.

Even though it was quiet, the woods in the distance didn't seem to be asleep. Strange cries echoed from across the lake—sad, desperate calls that didn't quite sound like owls or birds. Slowly, the sounds seemed to come closer, moving across the water and into the garden bushes. Then everything fell silent.

Just as Stephen was about to close the window and go back to reading Robinson Crusoe, he spotted two figures standing on the stone terrace below—the shapes of a boy and a girl. They stood still, side by side, staring up at the house. Something about the girl reminded him of the figure he had seen in his dream, the one in the bathtub. The boy filled him with a much deeper fear.

The girl stood calmly, hands folded over her chest, wearing a soft, almost sad smile. The boy, thin and ragged, with black hair and torn clothes, raised both arms high into the air. His pose felt threatening and full of hunger and pain. The moonlight made his hands almost glow, and Stephen could see that his fingernails were shockingly long and thin—the light actually passed through them. As the boy lifted his arms, something awful was revealed: a huge, dark tear in the left side of his chest. At that moment, Stephen didn't exactly hear a sound, but felt a horrible cry inside his head—the same kind of cry he'd heard coming from the woods earlier.

Then, as if floating, the boy and girl moved silently and quickly across the gravel. In seconds, they were gone.

Stephen was terrified, but he gathered his courage, lit a candle, and headed downstairs to Mr. Abney's study. Their meeting time was almost here. The study was just off the main hallway at the front of the house, and Stephen, afraid but determined, hurried there.

The door didn't seem to be locked—the key was still in place on the outside—but when he knocked several times, no one answered. He could hear Mr. Abney speaking inside, but not clearly. Then came something worse—he heard a voice cry out, suddenly cut off, as if choked. Stephen froze. Had Mr. Abney seen the ghostly children too?

The silence that followed was overwhelming. Stephen, now panicking, pushed hard on the door. This time, it opened.

***

When Stephen Elliott was old enough to understand, he read some papers that had been found on Mr. Abney's desk. These papers revealed everything. The most important parts said this:

"Long ago, people believed that certain rituals—though they might seem harsh or cruel to us now—could awaken powerful abilities in a person's spirit. They thought that by taking in the lives of others, a person could gain complete control over the spiritual forces that shape the world around us.

"One old story tells of a man named Simon Magus who could fly, turn invisible, or take on different shapes by using the soul of a boy he had 'killed'—though the old texts suggest that word might be too harsh. Another writer, Hermes Trismegistus, described how someone could gain the same powers by taking the hearts of three young people under the age of twenty-one. I've spent the past twenty years testing this idea, choosing people whose disappearance wouldn't draw too much attention.

"My first step was with Phoebe Stanley, a girl of gypsy background, on March 24, 1792. The second was a wandering Italian boy named Giovanni Paoli, taken on March 23, 1805. The final person must be my cousin, Stephen Elliott. His turn comes this March 24, 1812.

"To take in a person's spirit, the heart must be removed while they are still alive, turned to ashes, and mixed into about a pint of red wine—port is best. The bodies of the first two were hidden in places like an unused bathroom or the wine cellar. Sometimes the spirits of these people—what most call ghosts—can cause problems. But someone with a calm, logical mind, like myself, won't be bothered much by their weak attempts at revenge.

"I look forward with great excitement to the powerful life this experiment might bring me. If it works, not only will I be beyond the reach of human punishment, but I might also avoid death itself."

***

Mr. Abney was discovered in his chair with his head leaning back and his face twisted in a mix of anger, fear, and pain. On the left side of his chest was a terrible, torn wound that exposed his heart. His hands were clean, and the long knife on the table hadn't been used—it was spotless. The injury looked like it could have been made by a wild animal, maybe a big cat. The window in the study was open, and the coroner believed some kind of creature had come in and attacked him.

But after Stephen Elliott read the papers found in the study, he believed something very different had happened.

The End

Thank You for Reading

Dear Reader,

We hope this timeless classic has sparked your imagination and enriched your literary journey. Now that you've turned the final page, we want to share a vision for the future of reading—one where every classic you've ever wanted to explore is at your fingertips, in a format that best suits your life.

We'd like to invite you to gain immediate, unlimited digital & audiobook access to hundreds of the most treasured literary classics ever written—along with the option to secure deluxe paperback, hardcover & box set editions at printing cost. Together, we can spark a new global literary renaissance alongside our small, independent publishing house called "The Library of Alexandria."

Thousands of years ago, the Library of Alexandria stood as a beacon of knowledge—until it was lost to history. We aim to reignite that spirit of preservation and discovery right now, in the modern age—only this time, it's accessible to all, in every language and every format.

Picture a world where every timeless classic, novel, poem, or philosophical treatise is not only available to read but also updated for today's readers—modernized, translated into any language or dialect, and ready to enjoy in any format you choose, whether that is in an eBook, audiobook, paperback, or deluxe hardcover & box set version a printing cost.

By joining our movement to rebuild the modern Library of Alexandria, you become part of an unprecedented mission to offer:

- **Unlimited Audiobook & eBook Access** to the **Greatest Classics of All Time**

    Instantly explore thousands of legendary works, from Plato and Shakespeare to Jane Austen and Leo Tolstoy. All are instantly ready to read or listen to, giving you a complete literary universe at your fingertips.

- **Paperback & Deluxe Editions at Printing Costs:**

    Purchase any title in a paperback, deluxe hardbound, or deluxe boxset edition at printing costs, shipped right to your doorstep. Curate your personal library of Alexandria with editions worthy of display— crafted to last, designed to captivate, and delivered straight to your door.

- **Modern translations for Contemporary Readers in all languages and dialects**

  Discover a vast selection of classics reimagined in clear, current language—no more struggling with outdated phrases or obscure references. Next to the original versions, we aim to offer translations in as many languages and dialects as possible.

  As we continue our translation efforts and add new languages, readers everywhere can connect with these works as if they were written today. By bridging linguistic divides, you're contributing to ensuring that these timeless stories become more meaningful, accessible, and inspiring for people across the globe.

- **Your Personal Library of Alexandria:**

  Over the months and years, you'll curate a unique physical archive of classics—each volume a testament to your taste, curiosity, and love of knowledge. It's not just about owning books—it's about curating a cultural legacy you'll cherish and pass down for generations to come.

- **Join a Global Literary Renaissance:**

  Your support fuels an ongoing mission: allowing us to reinvest in offering deluxe print editions (including special boxsets) at their true cost, broaden the range of available formats and translations, and extend the reach of these works to new audiences worldwide. By joining today, you're not just preserving a legacy of masterpieces; you set in motion a powerful wave of literary accessibility.

We are more than a publisher—we're a movement, and we can't do it alone. Your support lets us scale our mission, preserving and reimagining history's greatest works for tomorrow's readers.

Become a Torchbearer of knowledge.

Thank you for picking up this book and allowing us into your literary journey. As you turn the pages, know that you're part of something larger: a global effort to keep these stories alive, share their wisdom across borders and generations, and spark a true cultural revival for the modern era.

If this resonates with you—please consider taking the next step by visiting:

www.libraryofalexandria.com

With gratitude and a shared love of knowledge,

The Modern Library of Alexandria Team

Visit:

www.libraryofalexandria.com

Or scan the code below: